PRODUCTION OVER PROFITS

BEGINNING A ROAD MAP TO A SUCCESSFUL FIXED OPERATIONS DEPARTMENT

The views and opinions expressed in this book are solely those of the author and do not reflect the views or opinions of Gatekeeper Press. Gatekeeper Press is not to be held responsible for and expressly disclaims responsibility of the content herein.

Production Over Profits

Published by Gatekeeper Press
2167 Stringtown Rd, Suite 109
Columbus, OH 43123-2989
www.GatekeeperPress.com

Copyright © 2021 by Chris Schaubert
All rights reserved. Neither this book, nor any parts within it may be sold or reproduced in any form or by any electronic or mechanical means, including information storage and retrieval systems, without permission in writing from the author. The only exception is by a reviewer, who may quote short excerpts in a review.

The interior formatting, typesetting, and editorial work for this book are entirely the product of the author. Gatekeeper Press did not participate in and is not responsible for any aspect of these elements.

Copyright for the images: iStockphoto.com/Macrovector (Car service composition), Duncan_Andison (Electronic gauge)

ISBN (paperback): 9781662919947

PRODUCTION OVER PROFITS

BEGINNING A ROAD MAP TO A SUCCESSFUL FIXED OPERATIONS DEPARTMENT

CHRIS SCHAUBERT

Columbus, Ohio

TABLE OF CONTENTS

INTRODUCTION...6

STRATEGY PAGES..8

TEAM...10

PRODUCTION...16

ABOUT THE AUTHOR.......................................22

INTRODUCTION

Before you close the book and think that I have lost my mind, please understand that I do not think that profit is a dirty word. To the contrary, I believe no one ever goes into business to lose money. That being said, my intent with this short book is to give the fixed operations world a new perspective.

Throughout my career, I have had continued success starting at the ground level and working my way up through variable and fixed operations. I have managed sales and fixed operations departments, and I have worked as a general manager. I have taken multiple fixed operations departments from a $30,000 or $50,000 monthly deficit to a profitable situation. Through my proven theory I can help you increase profits, employee retention, and customer satisfaction.

STRATEGY PAGE

STRATEGY PAGES

To the right of every written page you will see a strategy page. These allow you to consider strategies and continually think about your current situation. As you read this content, make notes about how you can make your business better and adjustments you can work towards making. Whoever is reading this book (from a service porter, detailer, technician, advisor, parts counter, to fixed ops director) it truly takes a team to work on these efforts. Let's collaborate together to take things to the next level.

We are indeed all in this together. Nothing else works.

STRATEGY PAGE

TEAM

The wrong leader can put you in a financially strained situation and make it appear that your department has a revolving door of employees. A team starts with an amazing leader. But the question to start out with first is, what is an amazing leader? Here are just a few characteristics that you must have to be an amazing leader:

1. You must be a great follower before you are an amazing leader.
2. You must be willing to do all that you are asking others to do.
3. You must be willing to jump in the trenches when needed.
4. You must understand that others are not the leader, you are.
5. You must have care and compassion. We live in a new time, with new problems and situations.

Those are just a few of the qualities of an amazing leader.

STRATEGY PAGE

You need to start to steer your mind to hold a team together. The culture that you instill in your fixed operations departments will start to show what kind of a team you will have. Ask yourself a few questions:

1. Have I done anything out of the ordinary to let my staff know I appreciate them? Or have I just cracked the whip and said that the paycheck should be thanks enough?

2. Have you noticed when an employee is having a rough day? Have you reached out to lend a hand or did you belittle them in front of their peers?

3. Have you hosted a complimentary lunch for everyone? You should be thinking about showing unity throughout the dealership.

4. Do you intentionally tell the owner or General Manager to give special recognition so that everyone can see that the owner or General Manager is involved and cares? After all, they are the top leaders in your establishment.

These are only a few examples of how you start to build a strong and positive culture in your departments.

You need to make sure that you are doing everything you can to show the team how you need it done. Instruct your employees in the right way and they will see that you, as a leader, want to lock arms with the team and take your department to the next level.

STRATEGY PAGE

Remember to be consistent with your meetings and with casting a vision. People want to be a part of something with direction and purpose. They need to continually hear this from you. Don't get so caught up in the money side that you forget about the people. If you are not careful then the employees become what you never wanted; they become a number and the family aspect of your business goes away. Then they start to feel that it is only about the money, production goes down, and less work gets through the shop.

STRATEGY PAGE

PRODUCTION

Production in your shop is the next step once you have made sure that a strong team and strong culture are in place. Production is like a chess game that you always need to be watching. Every step matters when you are talking about production. This is where the team efforts will pay off. How are your different positions working with each other?

Let's look at the steps of a customer coming into your service department. When your customer is entering the service department and they are greeted by a service greeter, a service porter, or a service advisor you need to look at the following steps. Do you have enough advisors? Is there a line of customers? Can your advisors effectively get the repair order written up and to the next location? Is there any help in busier times or are your express and main technicians sometimes waiting for repair orders in order to start working? After the repair order is written and the customer is in the waiting area or has left the dealership, what are your next steps?

STRATEGY PAGE

Where is the car parked and where are the keys placed? Where is the repair order placed? Is there a different process for a new customer or a returning customer who need to have their ordered parts replaced?

If the customer is returning for a replacement part, does the technician have to wait for the part from the parts counter or does someone else wait? Your technicians should have the parts brought to them, or at the very least you need to create a better process that you come up with to not have technicians wasting their time. Remember that some of you even have master technicians waiting at the parts counter and wasting valuable time they could use to make themselves and the department money.

Are you actively working as a team (including the management) throughout the day or are there many times where you hear "that's not my job?" How active are you as a leader or service advisor in your shop? Do you know when your technicians are 15 to 20 minutes from finishing a job so that you can make sure that you have everything ready for their next job? Do you ask the technician regularly about their progress, not to nag them, but to show that you care.

Side note: Be careful to avo[id] thinking that hiring a superst[ar] advisor or great master technici[an] will solve all your problems. If y[ou] do not have production process[es] in place and monitor them close[ly] then they will not be able to get t[he] work they are selling or executi[ng] through the shop efficiently.

In this case, they might g[et] frustrated and leave because y[ou] promised them there was mo[re] work then they would kn[ow] what to do with, but can not g[et] it completed. Furthermore, th[ey] might not be making the mon[ey] you promised them, so th[ey] get frustrated from your lack [of] leadership and leave.

STRATEGY PAGE

You would be surprised at how much frustration is added throughout the day in your departments because people feel like nobody cares. If you help make others more money, they will in turn make you more financial gain.

People, employees, partners, and team members all need to see that you care. When they see that you care, they work more efficiently; they think smarter because there is greater communication and collaboration. They trust your words and see you as helping versus demanding. Most employees in fixed operations are on some sort of bonus or incentive plan for production, so do you help them become better? Do they feel and see that from you? There are many areas for improvement in every fixed operations department. Let's help each other grow!

STRATEGY PAGE

ABOUT THE AUTHOR

Chris Schaubert is an expert in fixed operations. He is passionate about helping dealerships improve their bottom line and customer experience. He will help you improve back-end processes and increase employee satisfaction and retention.

Founder of Fixed Ops Solutions, Chris began his career in the automotive industry over ten years ago. Now, Chris is confidently familiar with all aspects of a dealership and where opportunities lie to improve operations and the bottom line. It was just prior to becoming a general manager that Chris was a fixed operations director. Being in fixed operations gave him a huge respect for the hard-working people of the automotive industry: the people turning wrenches, helping customers, and writing up tickets for customers. He gained knowledge on how to operate more efficiently, create more production, and move more product in a way that builds a better culture and experience for the employees while also gaining profits for the dealership. Chris now takes that knowledge and shares it with his clients and as a speaker at industry conferences.

STRATEGY PAGE

Thank you for taking the time to read through this content. Hopefully it has stirred your mind to start thinking towards better processes, culture, and activity throughout your fixed operations departments. Although writing ideas down on a page is a great step, remember that they need to be put into action. I know that things can get busy throughout the day and many times good intentions do not take root. That being said, if myself or my team can help be of assistance to you, please do not hesitate to contact us. We look forward to partnering up and serving you and your team.

STRATEGY PAGE

Made in the USA
Las Vegas, NV
23 July 2024

92811006R00015